D1636158

Compass Rose

Books by Arthur Sze

POETRY

Compass Rose

The Ginkgo Light

Quipu

The Redshifting Web: Poems 1970   1998

Archipelago

River River

Dazzled

Two Ravens

The Willow Wind

TRANSLATIONS

The Silk Dragon: Translations from the Chinese

EDITOR

Chinese Writers on Writing

ARTHUR SZE | Compass Rose

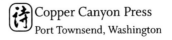
Copper Canyon Press
Port Townsend, Washington

Copper Canyon Press is in residence at Fort Worden State Park
in Port Townsend, Washington, under the auspices of Centrum.
Centrum is a gathering place for artists and creative thinkers
from around the world, students of all ages and backgrounds,
and audiences seeking extraordinary cultural enrichment.

LIBRARY OF CONGRESS CATALOGING IN PUBLICATION DATA

Sze, Arthur.
[Poems. Selections]
Compass Rose / Arthur Sze.
pages cm.
Includes bibliographical references.
ISBN 978 1 55659 467 0
I. Title.
PS3569.Z38C66 2014
811.54   dc23
            2013025678

Copper Canyon Press
Post Office Box 271
Port Townsend, Washington 98368

www.coppercanyonpress.org

for Carol
for Micah and Sarah

Contents

Compass Rose

Black kites with outstretched wings circle overhead—

After a New Moon

Each evening you gaze in the southwest sky
as a crescent extends in argentine light.
When the moon was new, your mind was
desireless, but now both wax to the world.
While your neighbor's field is cleared,
your corner plot is strewn with desiccated
sunflower stalks. You scrutinize the bare
apricot limbs that have never set fruit,
the wisteria that has never blossomed,
and wince, hearing how, at New Year's,
teens bashed in a door and clubbed strangers.
Near a pond, someone kicks a dog out
of a pickup. Each second, a river edged
with ice shifts course. Last summer's
exposed tractor tire is nearly buried
under silt. An owl lifts from a poplar,
while the moon, no, the human mind
moves from brightest bright to darkest dark.

Sticking out of yellow-tongued flames on a ghat, a left foot—

Near a stopped bus, one kid performs acrobatics while another drums—

The Curvature of Earth

Red beans in a flat basket catch sunlight—

we enter a village built in the shape
of an ox, stride up an arched bridge

over white lilies; along houses, water,
coursing in alleyways, connects ponds.

Kiwis hang from branches by a moon

door. We step into a two-story hall
with a light well and sandalwood panels:

in a closet off the mahjong room
is a bed for clandestine encounters.

A cassia tree shades a courtyard

corner; phoenix-tail bamboos line
the horse-head walls. The branching

of memory resembles these interconnected
waterways: a chrysanthemum odor

permeates the air, but I can't locate it.

Soldiers fire mortars at enemy bunkers,
while Afghan farmers pause then resume

slicing poppy bulbs and draining resin.
A caretaker checks on his clients' lawns

and swimming pools. The army calls—

he swerves a golf cart into a ditch—
the surf slams against black lava rock,

against black lava rock—and a welt
spreads across his face. Hunting for

a single glow-in-the-dark jigsaw piece,

we find incompletion a spark.
We volley an orange Ping-Pong ball

back and forth: hungers and fears
spiral through us, forming a filament

by which we heat into cesium light.

And, in the flowing current, we slice
back and forth—topspin, sidespin—

the erasure of history on the arcing ball.
Snow on the tips of forsythia dissolves

within hours. A kestrel circles overhead,

while we peer into a canyon and spot
caves but not a macaw petroglyph.

Yesterday, we looked from a mesa tip
across the valley to Chimayó, tin roofs

glinting in sunlight. Today, willows

extend one-inch shoots; mourning cloaks
flit along the roadside; a red-winged

blackbird calls. Though the March world
leafs and branches, I ache at how

mortality fissures the lungs:

and the pangs resemble ice forming,
ice crystals, ice that resembles the wings

of cicadas, ice flowers, drift ice, ice
that forms at the edges of a rock

midstream, thawing hole in ice, young

shore ice, crack in ice caused by the tides.
Scissors snip white chrysanthemum stalks—

auburn through a black tea-bowl rim—
is water to Siberian irises as art

is to life? You have not taken care

of tying your shoes—a few nanoseconds,
a few thousand years—water catlaps

up the Taf Estuary to a boathouse—
herring shimmer and twitch in a rising net—

rubbing blackthorn oil on her breasts—

in a shed, words; below the cliff, waves—
where *å i åa ä e ö* means *island in the river*—

while a veteran rummages through trash,
on Mars, a robot arm digs for ice—

when the bow lifts from the D string,

"This is no way to live," echoes in his ears.
Sandhill cranes call from the marsh,

then, low, out of the southwest,
three appear and drop into the water:

their silhouettes sway in the twilight,

the marsh surface argentine and black.
Before darkness absorbs it all, I recall

locks inscribed with lovers' names
on a waist-high chain extending along

a path at the top of Yellow Mountain.

She brushes her hair across his chest;
he runs his tongue along her neck—

reentering the earth's atmosphere,
a satellite ignites. A wavering line

of cars issues north out of the bosque.

The last shapes of cranes dissolve
into vitreous darkness. Setting aside

binoculars, I adjust the side-view
mirror—our breath fogs the windshield.

A complex of vibrating strings:

this hand, that caress, this silk
gauze running across your throat,

your eyelids, this season where
tiny ants swarm large black ones

and pull apart their legs. Hail shreds

the rows of lettuces beyond the fence;
water, running through sprinklers,

swirls. A veteran's wince coincides
with the pang a girl feels when

she masters hooked bows in a minuet.

And the bowing is a curved line,
loop, scrawl, macaw in air. A red-

winged blackbird nests in the dark;
where we pruned branches, starlight

floods in over the earth's curvature.

Begging near a car window, a girl with a missing arm—

Mynah bird sipping water out of a bronze bowl sprinkled with jasmine petals—

Twitching before he plays a sarangi near the temple entrance, a blind man—

Compass Rose

1 ARCTIC CIRCLE

If the strings of a ¾ violin
are at rest, if the two horsehair
bows repose in their case—
the case holds the blue of lakes
and the whites of snow;
she posts on a horse inside a barn;
rain splatters on the skylight
during the night; she inhales
the smell of newly born chickens
in a stall—if the interval
between lightning and thunder
is a blue dagger, if she hears
Gavotte in D Major as he drives
in silence past Camel Rock—
she stirs then drifts into feathered
waves of sleep; a healer rebuilds
her inner moon and connection
to the earth while she plays
Hangman with her mother;
she stops running out into the cold
whirlpool dark; behind his eyelids,
green curtains of light shimmer
across the polar sky; she has difficulty
posting with one foot in the stirrup—
if he stands, at minus fifteen degrees,
a black dot in the snow—she rides
bareback to regain her balance;
he prays that diverging rays

emanate from a single quartz crystal;
he prays that her laughter be
June grass, that the jagged floating
chunks of ice ease and dissolve;
he prays when she lights a tiny
candle on a shelf; reindeer eat
lichens and browse among marshes
at the height of summer—
if she bows and hears applause
then puts her bow to the string,
if she decides, "This is nothing,"
let the spark ignite horse become
barn become valley become world.

He pours water into a cup: at room temperature,
the cup is white, but, after he microwaves it,

and before steeping a tea bag with mint leaves,
he notices outlines of shards have formed

above the water. As the cup cools, the lines
disappear: now he glimpses fault lines

inside himself and feels a Siberian tiger
pace along the bars of a cell—black, orange,

white; black, orange, white—and feels how
the repeating chord sends waves through him.

His eyes glisten, and he tries to dispel the crests,
but *what have I done, what can I do* throbs

in his arteries and veins. Today he will
handle plutonium at the lab and won't

consider beryllium casings. He situates the past
in the slight aroma of mint rising in the air.

Sometimes he feels like an astronaut suspended
above Earth twisting on an umbilical cord;

sometimes he's in the crosshairs of a scope,
and tiger stripes flow in waves across his body.

Red-winged blackbirds in the cattail pond—
today I kicked an elk hoof off the path,
read that armadillo eaters can catch
leprosy, but who eats armadillo and eats
it rare? Last night you wrote that, walking
to the stables, you glimpsed horses at twilight
in a field. We walk barefoot up a ridge
and roll down a dune; sip raki, savor
shish kebab and yogurt in an arcade.
Once we pored over divination lines incised
into tortoise shells, and once we stepped
through the keyhole entry into a garden
with pools of glimmering water. In the gaps
between my words, peonies rise through hoops
behind our bedroom—peonies are indeed
rising through hoops behind our bedroom—
you comb your hair at the sink as they unfold.

4 ORCHID HOUR

Orchid leaves are dark against the brighter glass;
two translucent blooms expand at the tip

of a segmented stalk, and, through the window,
an orange hue limns the Jemez Mountains.

At the lab a technician prepares a response
to a hypothetical anthrax attack, and what

is imagined can be: lionfish proliferate
in the Caribbean, traces of uranium appear

in an aquifer, and the beads of an abacus
register a moment in time: the cost of cabbage,

catfish crammed in a bubbling tank—and words
in the dictionary are spores: *xeriscape, fugu,*

cloister, equanimity. In the orchid hour,
you believe you know where you are, looking

before and through a window, but a pang lodges—
out of all the possible worlds, this, this.

5   THE CURTAIN

Inside each galaxy is a black hole—
         we will never see your birth mother's face—
our solar system has eight, not nine, planets—
         we will never know the place of your birth—
who anticipated five dwarf planets
         in our solar system
         or that ice lodged on one of Jupiter's moons?

When three caretakers brought three babies
         into the room, your mother leapt out of her chair,
         knowing at a glance your face.
We do not want anyone to be like the rings of Saturn,
         glinting in orbit,
         or inhabiting the gaps between rings;
we do not want anyone to be like Uranus.

On a whiteboard, you draw a heart, an infinity sign,
         star, and attune to a gyroscope's tilt.
At night I've pulled the curtain
and stopped at the point
         where you twirled and transfixed—
         but tonight I pull the curtain to the end:
inside our planet is a molten core.

6 2'33"

Land mines in fields are waiting to explode—
from the right lane, a car zips ahead:

you brake, and as it brakes into a left-
turn bay, you glance at the movie marquee

and twenty-four-hour grocery store:
at a checkout counter, a clerk scans

an eight-pack of AA batteries, asks
if you're playing Monopoly; no, no,

and tonight you're lucky: you don't need
a kidney transplant; no one angles a shiv

at your throat—a farmer hesitates
to pace a field before planting yams—

his father's leg tore in a gunpowder burst—
along the riverbed, you spot a few beer

bottles and tire tracks but no elk carcass
in the brush: no snarling dogs leap out—

Orion pulses above the Sangre de Cristos—
and you plunge into highway darkness ahead.

7   COMET HYAKUTAKE

Comet Hyakutake's tail stretches for 360 million miles—

in 1996, we saw Hyakutake through binoculars—

the ion tail contains the time we saw bats emerge out of a cavern at dusk—

in the cavern, we first heard stalactites dripping—

first silence, then reverberating sound—

our touch reverberates and makes a blossoming track—

a comet's nucleus emits X-rays and leaves tracks—

two thousand miles away, you box up books and, in two days, will step
      through the invisible rays of an airport scanner—

we write on invisible pages in an invisible book with invisible ink—

in nature's book, we read a few pages—

in the sky, we read the ion tracks from the orchard—

the apple orchard where blossoms unfold, where we unfold—

budding, the child who writes, "the puzzle comes to life"—

elated, puzzled, shocked, dismayed, confident, loving: minutes to
      an hour—

a minute, a pinhole lens through which light passes—

Comet Hyakutake will not pass Earth for another 100,000 years—

no matter, ardor is here—

and to the writer of fragments, each fragment is a whole—

Red-winged blackbirds in the cattail pond—
today I kicked and flipped a wing
in the sand and saw it was a sheared-
off flicker's. Yesterday's rain has left

snow on Tesuque Peak, and the river
will widen then dwindle. We step
into a house and notice antlers mounted
on the wall behind us; a ten-day-old child

looks, nurses, and sleeps; his mother
smiles but says she cries then cries
as emptiness brims up and over.
And as actions are rooted in feelings,

I see how picking spinach in a field
blossoms the picker, how a thoughtless act
shears a wing. As we walk out
to the car, the daylight is brighter

than we knew. We do not believe
flames shoot out of a cauldron of days
but, looking at the horizon, see
flames leap and crown from tree to tree.

9 COMPASS ROSE

Along the ridge, flames leaped and crowned
from tree to tree. We woke to charred pine
needles in the yard; smoke misted then hazed
the orchard. What closes and is literal,
what opens and is figurative? A healer aligns
her east and west, her north and south.
They backfired fires against the larger blaze—
barrels of plutonium on the mesa in white tents.
We do not circumnavigate but pinhole through it.
She leads a horse past stalls; what closes
and is figurative, what opens and is literal?
Through the skylight she watches a rising moon.
The lines hold, and the fire sweeps south
and north. Sometimes a thistle is just
a thistle. We step out of the sauna and take
a cold plunge; cottonwoods in the riverbed
form a curved flame. Through here,
water cascades; she posts a horse into daylight.

Shaggy red clouds in the west—

unlatching a gate, I step into a field:
        no coyote slants across with a chicken in its mouth,

        no wild asparagus rises near the ditch.

In the night sky, Babylonian astronomers
        recorded a supernova
        and witnessed the past catch up to the present,

        but they did not write
                what they felt at what they saw—

they could not see to this moment.
From August, we could not see to this moment

        but draw water out of a deep well—
        it has the taste of

        creek water in a tin cup,
                and my teeth ache against the cold.

Juniper smoke rises and twists through the flue—

        my eyes widen
        as I brush your hair, brush your hair—

I have red breath:
in the deep night, we are again lit,
          and I true this time to consequence.

In relief, a naked woman arches and pulls a thorn out of her raised heel—

Men carry white-wrapped corpses on bamboo stretchers down the steps—

She undresses: a scorpion on her right thigh—

A boy displays a monkey on a leash then smacks it with a stick—

Available Light

1

Sandalwood-scented flames engulf a corpse—
farther down the ghat, a man carries fire
in his right hand to a shaved body placed
faceup on logs. He circles five times, ignites
the pyre: the dead man's mouth opens.
Moored offshore, we rock in a creaking skiff,
stiffen at these fires which engulf lifetimes.
A fine soot hangs in the air; in a hotel room,
a woman infected with typhoid writhes,
"Do not let me die," and a doctor's assistant
injects her with antibiotics. Today, no one
comprehends how dark energy and dark
matter enlace this world; no one stares
at the heart-shaped leaves of spring
and infers we are ensnared by our illusions.
After someone cuts the barbed wire across
the arroyo, three-wheelers slash ruts into slopes.

2

Huddled by roadside fires—

"In the end, we're dust streamers
ionized by ultraviolet radiation"—

teens ditch school and ransack mailboxes—

along the dark street, an elephant lumbers—

cracking a skull with a hammer—

a Yield sign riddled with bullet holes—

metastasized to his brain—

gazing in each other's eyes,
they flow and overflow—

a one-legged girl at a car window.

3

Along a sculptured sandstone wall, a dancer
raises a right foot to fasten ankle bells;

a naked woman arches and scrubs her back;
a flute player wets his lips and blows.

We try to sleep, but a rat scavenges
on the floor; at dawn, pulling a curtain,

you find a showerhead wrapped in plastic,
crank the faucet: red-brown water gurgles out.

Theriomorphic gods pass through the mind,
but an egret may be an egret. Pausing

at a bomb alert on a glass door, I scan cars
jammed into the square; you hand alms

to a one-eyed woman, whiff red chiles
in burlap sacks. Soldiers cordon off a gate,

set rifles with inverted-V mounts on sandbags.
At dusk, someone on a motorcycle throws

acid at two women and grabs a purse.
A woman wraps a leg around her lover;

dressed only in gold foil, a man gesticulates—
we wipe soot off the backs of our necks.

4

By the acequia headgate, a rib cage—

smoking in a wheelchair,
she exhales and forms a rafflesia flower—

pit bull on a leash—

all men are mortal—

he set his Laundromat ablaze—

the rising spires resembling Himalayan peaks—

"I cannn't talk"—

parrots squawking in the branches of an ashoka tree—

heat death—

when is recollection liberation?

5

Streamers around a bodhi tree, the elongated
leaf tips; under an eave, the hexagonal cells
of a wasp nest. With a wheelbarrow, someone
hauls mixed clay and sand to waiting men.
Once I tilted hawk and trowel, plastered cement
on walls, ran metal lath across the setting coat.
"Their gold teeth and rings burn with their bodies,"
says the boatman. Our love cries vanish into air,
yet my tongue running along your clavicle
releases spring light in the room. Our fingertips
floodgate open: death, no, ardor will be violet
flare to our nights, and the knots of existence
dissolve when we no longer try to grasp them.
The net of the past dissolves when the mixer
stops mixing: cranes stalk fish in shallow ponds;
a woman aligns basil plants in terra-cotta pots;
out of nowhere, a fly strikes a windowpane.

6

At a rink, you step onto ice and mark the lines
already cut, but they are not your lines;
the mind pools what will happen with
what has happened. Moving out and
cutting an arc, you find the locus of creation.
You do not need to draw "nine"
and "four" in ashes to end your attachment
to the dead; you yearn to live as a river
fans out in a delta. A man tosses a pot
of water behind his shoulder and releases
the dark energy of attachment; fires recede
into darkness and become candlelights
bobbing downstream. In this hourglass place,
ants lift grains of sand above brickwork,
creating a series of circular dunes;
two baby robins sleep behind wisteria leaves;
in an attosecond, *here* and *there* dissolve.

7

Lifting off a cottonwood, a red-tailed hawk—
carved in a sandstone wall, a woman applies

henna to her right hand. By the papaya tree,
we climb to a rooftop, peer down at wheat

spread out on another roof—pink and madder
clothes pinned to a line in a backyard.

A bull with a swishing tail lumbers past
the flashlight store; and what is complex

is most simple. In a doorway, a girl leaning
into sunshine writes on the stone floor.

We sip chai in a courtyard, inhale the aroma
of neem leaves laced with diesel exhaust.

I hose new grass by the kitchen, guess
to be liberated from the past is to be

freed from the future; and, as sunlight
inclines, making the bougainvillea leaves

by the window translucent, I catch
our fugitive, living tracks as we make our way.

The Infinity Pool

Someone snips barbed wire and gathers
yerba mansa in the field; the Great Red Spot

on Jupiter whirls counterclockwise;
sea turtles beach on white sand. In the sky,

a rose hue floats over a blue that limns
a deeper blue at the horizon. Unwrapping

chewing gum, a child asks, "Where
is the end to matter?" Over time, a puffer

fish evolved resistance to tetrodotoxin
and synthesized it. I try on T-shirts

from a shelf, but not, twenty months later,
your father's pajamas in the drawer.

Now the stiletto palm-leaves are delineated,
a yellow-billed cardinal sips at a ledge.

By long count, a day's a drop in an infinity
pool. The rose tips of clouds whiten;

someone sprinkles crushed mica into clay
and sand before plastering an interior wall.

Strike-Slip

Faucets drip, and the night plunges to minus
    fifteen degrees. Today you stared at a map
of Africa on a school wall and shook your head
    at "Yugoslavia" written along the Adriatic
coast near the top—how many times
    are lines drawn and redrawn, and to what end?

This ebony bead yours, that amber one
    another's. A coelacanth swims in the depths
off Mozambique and eludes a net; a crystal
    layer forms behind your retinas. Today
you saw the long plastic sheet in the furrow
    blown, like a shroud, around elm branches.

A V-shaped aquatic-grass cutter leans
    against the porch, and you ponder how things
get to where they are. A young writer
    from Milwaukee who yearned to travel calls—
he's hiked the Himalayas and frets
    at what to do: in Nepal, during civil strife,

he and an Israeli backpacker smoked
    and yakked all night in the emptied hotel;
now that the snow is dissolving off Everest,
    bodies of climbers and trash are exposed.
A glowing eel in the darkness—anguish.
    He clacks the beads, *how to live, where to go.*

She wrings her hair after stepping out of a bath—

A portion of a leograph visible amid rubble—

A woman averts her gaze from the procession of war elephants—

Two boys at a car window receive red apples—

Sipping masala tea in an inner courtyard with blue-washed walls—

The Immediacy of Heat

1

No Trespassing is nailed to a cottonwood trunk,
but the sign vanishes within days. You've seen

a pile of sheep bones dumped off the dirt road
to the river; in the arroyo, you've heard gunshots

and veered upstream. On the highway, a pickup
tailgates a new car, and red plastic flowers,

at a curve, fade. In the slanted rising light,
men stumble out of brambles along the bosque

and head into town; and you time your trip
to the drugstore so you aren't accosted

by women hungering for a fix. At the high school,
chains are drawn above the pavement;

the casino parking lot is already dotted with cars.
At the adjoining bowling alley, someone hurls

a strike, and, inside, you lose track of spring.
You catch the clatter of coins—people

blank into themselves. Searching for an exit,
you find you've zigzagged and circled a maze.

2

At the mesa's brink, we eye the road
snaking across the valley toward Pedernal,
where hunters gathered flint. A new moon
and two planets bob in the deepening sky;
I lean into the wind and find this tension
the beginning of a sphere. I bend to a stone
basin and, ladling water, sip. I'm lit
and feel new leaves slide out of branches;
see a child, gathering blue pine needles,
inhale the aroma of earth; a worker
snips and nails metal lath into a firewall.
At our first talk, time grew rounded:
a sparkler scattered sparks in all directions—
though gone, they're gone into my fingertips.
The beauty of imperfection's when a potter
slightly pinches a bowl while arcing it
into a second glaze so that, fired,
the bowl marks a crescent hare's-fur overlay.

3

Under a microscope, I once gazed at algae, at cork cells—

bald eagles at the end of a pier—

a sheep carcass near an arroyo's mouth—

he plants lettuces in the field, and that night it snows—

a woman has closed her eyelids and will never reopen them—

a crow alights on a branch—

the crunching sounds of inlet ice breaking up—

six cars in the driveway—

the invisible lines of isobars, always shifting—

one thing it is to focus; another, to twig—

some of the plastered exterior walls lack the final color coat—

flowering dogwood—

the circular saw rang out through the cambium of summer—

when she vanishes, he will shiver and shiver—

4

Stepping out of the casino, you blink, but lights
still ricochet off glass. *Do not take checks*

from Samantha Cruz is posted on a billboard
by the liquor warehouse. Disorientation's

a rope burn in your hands: are we green flies
drawn to stinkhorns? or shoots leafing

out of time's branches? You blink:
someone hurls a grenade but detonates

himself. You blink: someone in the hallway
at the Bureau of Indian Affairs shouts, "Fire me."

You blink, and a profusion of lavender enters
the window. Dipping under incoming waves,

you resurface with a salt sting on your eyelids.
Once you scavenged a burn for morels.

An unemployed carpenter builds his daughter
a harp; you catch yearning, love, solace

as the forty-six strings are tightened.
You can't pluck them, but the emotions mesh.

5

Vibrating strings
  compose matter and force—
    as I run a magnetic card

  at a subway turnstile, a wave
of people converges and flows
    through the gates; people will always

converge and flow
  through the gates—always?
    If I sprinkle iron filings onto a sheet

of paper, I make visible
  the magnetic lines of the moment.
    At closing hour,

the manager of a restaurant
  sweats and anticipates a dark figure
    bursting in and aiming

  a gun at his chest, but tonight
no figure appears. In this world,
    we stare at a rotating needle

  on a compass and locate
by closing our eyes. At dusk
    our fingertips are edged with light,

the fifty-four bones of our hands
are edged with light,

and the immediacy of heat
is a spring melt among conifers
gathering into a cascade.

At the Equinox

The tide ebbs and reveals orange and purple sea stars.
I have no special theory of radiance,

      but after rain evaporates
off pine needles, the needles glisten.

In the courtyard, we spot the rising shell of a moon,
and, at the equinox, bathe in its gleam.

Using all the tides of starlight,
      we find
      vicissitude is our charm.

On the mudflats off Homer,
I catch the tremor when waves start to slide back in;

and, from Roanoke, you carry
      the leafing jade smoke of willows.

Looping out into the world, we thread
      and return. The lapping waves

cover an expanse of mussels clustered on rocks;
and, giving shape to what is unspoken,

      forsythia buds and blooms in our arms.

Returning to Northern New Mexico
after a Trip to Asia

A tea master examines pellets with tweezers,
points to the varying hues, then pushes
the dish aside. At another shop, a woman
rinses a cylindrical cup with black tea:
we inhale, nod, sip from a second cup—
rabbit tracks in snow become tracks
in my mind. At a banquet, eating something
sausage-like, I'm told, "It's a chicken's ball."
Two horses huddle under leafless poplars.
A neighbor runs water into an oval container,
but, in a day, the roan bangs it with his hoof.
The skunks and raccoons have vanished.
What happened to the End World Hunger project?
Revolutionary slogans sandblasted off
Anhui walls left faint outlines. When
wind swayed the fragrant pine branches
in a Taiwan garden, Sylvie winced, "Kamikaze
pilots drank and whored their last nights here."

Qiviut

A dog's bark has use, and so does honey
and a harpoon. The Inuit use the undercoat

wool of the musk ox, qiviut, to make
scarves and hats. The unexpected utility

of things is a calculus: a wooden spoon,
in a ceramic jar by the stove, has flavors

and stains from tomatoes and garlic,
cilantro and potato broth; it has nicks

and scorch lines, the oil of human hands.
Aspirin may be sifted out of willow bark,

but of what use, other than to the butterfly,
are a butterfly's wings? The weight

of a pin is equivalent to a hundred
postage stamps, and words, articulated

with care, may heal a rift across waters.
An unspoken pang may, like an asymptote,

approach visible speech: it runs closer
and closer but does not touch. As it

runs out of sight, words are mulled:
Venus, a black speck, flies across the sun.

Backlit

You pick the next-to-last apple off a branch;
here's to ripening, to the bur that catches
on your shoelace and makes you pause,

consider, retrace your path. The cottonwoods
have burst into yellow flame; by the ditch,
someone dumps a pile of butchered bones.

When we saw white droppings on the brick porch,
we turned and looked up to five screech owls
roosting on a dark beam, backlit

through wisteria leaves. By the metal gate,
a bobcat bounds off with a rabbit in his mouth.
You yearn to watch sunlight stream

through the backs of Japanese maples
but see sheet lightning in the dark—
it flows from your toes to fingertips to hair.

An aura reader jots down the colors of your seven chakras—

A bus hits a motorcycle from behind and runs over the driver and his
    passenger—

Discussing the price of a miniature elephant on wheels—

Green papayas on a tree by a gate—

Lit candles bobbing downstream into the sinuous darkness—

A naked woman applies kohl to her right eyelid—

The limp tassels of new ashoka leaves in a tomb courtyard—

Confetti

Strike, rub, crumple—rip paper into shreds:
you can make confetti form a quick orange
blossom before it collapses to the ground.
At night, a driver misses a curve and plows
through the wall into a neighbor's dining room;
twice a day, another neighbor breaks apart
ice with a pick, and her horses dip their heads
into the tub. At dawn, branches scrape,
like rough flint, against the window;
where I stare, a woman once threw a shuttle
back and forth through the alternating sheds
at her loom, and that sound was a needle
sparking through emptiness. Last night,
as sleet hit the skylight, we moved from
trough to crest to radiating wave: even as
shrapnel litters the ground, as a car flips
and scatters bright shards of CDs into the grass.

Spectral Hues

The Chandra telescope tracks
    a particle's X-ray emissions
        before it vanishes into a black hole,

but pin your eyes to earth.
    At sixty, you do not hunger
        to spot an iridescent green

butterfly alighting on moss—
    shift your eyes and it's there.
        A great blue heron lands

on a pond island, and all
    emotions vibrate in spectral
        hues inside the totality

of white light. Driving toward
    the Los Alamos mesas,
        you pass a yellow spot,

where a cottonwood was chainsawed
    after they found
        their son dangling from a limb.

You sprinkle dragon well leaves
    in a glass cup, add simmering water,
        and, when the leaves

unfurl, pour some off, add more,
    sip: now mortality's
        a wave, a trampoline into light.

Windows and Mirrors

Ladybug moving along a cast-iron chair—
translucent pink of a budding lotus
in the pond—you slide along
a botanical wall, recall someone

who stammered to avoid the army
and then could not undo his stutter.
A wasp lays eggs in a tarantula;
a gecko slips under the outdoor grill.

You bite into a deep-fried scorpion
on a skewer: when your father reached
for the inhaler, your mother
stopped breathing. Iridescent green

butterflies pinned to the wall—
a rainbow passing across an island—
striding past ants on a bougainvillea,
you find windows and mirrors

in the refractive index of time.
Tracks of clothes on the floor—
white plumeria on the grass—
hatched wasps consume the tarantula.

Midnight Loon

Burglars enter an apartment and ransack drawers;
finding neither gold nor cash, they flee,

leaving the laundry and bathroom lights on—
they have fled themselves. I catch the dipping

pitch of a motorcycle, iceberg hues in clouds;
the gravel courtyard's a midnight garden,

as in Japan, raked to resemble ocean waves
in moonshine, whirlpool eddies, circular ripples—

and nothing is quite what it appears to be.
When I unlatch the screen door, a snake

slides under the weathered decking; I spot
the jagged hole edged with glass where a burglar

reached through the window, but no one
marks the poplars darker with thunder and rain.

In moonlight I watch the whirlpool hues
of clouds drift over our courtyard, adobe walls,

and gate, and, though there is no loon,
a loon calls out over the yard, over the water.

Point-Blank

Through the irregular mesh of a web,
you shove an inverted vase down
but, instead of trapping a black widow,
squash it when the glass strikes
the floor. Put your fingers
on the mind's strings: in the silence,
you do not grasp silence—a thoughtless
thought permeates you. In Medellín,
a man recalls faces but can't recall
what he wrote or said last night; fretting
at the widening chasm, he runs from X
but does not know if he lunges
this way or to his end. Lifting the vase,
you examine spider legs on the brick floor,
the bulk of the black widow smeared
inside the glass. *A yesterday like today,*
he wrote, and, in his point-blank gaze,
for a second, you are a spider in a web.

The Radius of Touch

Rising over granite cliffs in an aerial tram,
we view the rippling lights of Albuquerque
and volcanoes to the west. At the summit,

the circumference of peaks dissolves
when I blink; and here I am, at a point
where all lines diverge. In the leafless dark,

I can't spot the branches of the golden
rain tree; in the kingdom of touch,
a candle flickers then steadies flame.

Some days are windblown sand stinging
my eyes; others, rice grains in a glass jar.
As matsutake mycelium mantles the roots

of red pine, our cries enmesh each other.
Suspended on cables, we rise up through
the moist darkening air, but the molten

wax of this space dissolves distance.
In the kingdom of scents, the chanterelle
patch we stumbled into flowers again,

and, when I blink, all lines converge.

A cobra rises out of a straw basket before a man plays a bulbous instrument—

Corpses consumed by flames and in all stages of burning—

The elongated tip of a bodhi leaf—

Arranged in a star pattern on a white plate, five dates—

On a balcony, in the darkness, smokers staring at a neem tree—

His head golden, and his sex red—

A naked woman gazing at herself in a small, circular mirror—

At sunrise, a girl rummages through ashes with tongs—

Along the river, men and women scrub clothes on stones—

The Unfolding Center

1

Tea leaves in a black bowl:
> *green snail spring* waiting to unfurl.
>> Nostrils flared, I inhale:

expectancy's a seed—
> we planted two rows
>> of sunflowers then drove to Colorado—

no one could alter the arrival
> of the ambulance,
>> the bulged artery; I had never

seen one hundred crows
> gathered at the river,
>> vultures circling overhead;

I saw no carcass, smelled no rot;
> the angers radiating from him
>> like knives in sunlight; I sit

at a river branching off a river:
> three vultures on cottonwood branches
> track my movement;

surrounded by weeds, I cut
> two large sunflower heads off
>> six-foot stalks, Apache plume

blossoms near the gate; we wake
      and embrace, embrace and wake,
          my fingers meshed

with your fingers. Nostrils flared,
      I inhale: time, *time*
          courses through the bowl of my hands.

2

A black-chinned hummingbird chick
angles beak and tail out of a nest
woven of spiderwebs and lichens.
Mature, it will range a thousand
miles between coast and highland.
Once you roamed a spice market for chai,
gazed into a mausoleum's keyhole entry
and discovered in synaptic memories
linkages that smoke, linkages that flower.
The owls never returned to the hole
high up the arroyo bank: each spring
clusters of wild irises rise in the field.
Leaning on a cedar bench, we view
fireworks bursting into gold arrays
and tilt on the outgoing tide of breath.
Fireflies brighten the darkening air:
desire's manifest here, here, and here's
the infinite in the intervening emptiness.

3

—Damn, I'm walking on the roof of hell, I need
       a smoke, I'm NOT a procrastinator, this sling

nags me, where's ~~my arm won't budge~~ my lighter?
       I hobble, fidget, can't drive, I'm a piece of shit

if I can't cast overhead *and unspool that speckled*
       fly onto blue flowing water; damn I miss

that bend in the Pecos, I crave Bolivia: when I lift
       that serape out of the trunk and *finger*

the cochineal-dyed weft and reach that slit at the neck,
       my mind floods, and I need to hang;

I need another drag, at night if my toes
       can't *wiggle* out of the sheets and relax,

I can't sleep, and if I can't sleep, I can't ~~fly fish~~ be—
       I'm going to a lodge near Traverse Bay

where a stream *shimmers* with ~~cutthroats~~ rainbow trout;
       why, I'm shrinking inside this body,

~~let me out,~~ it's fucking paradise here,
       I'll go back in and, after *I needle that willow*

into that Apache basket, ~~under the overhead lights~~
       ~~I won't have to squint,~~ it will all be repaired—

4

I slice oyster mushrooms off an aspen
then, in the next clearing, stumble
into beer cans and plastic bags.
We cannot elude ourselves; we jump
across state lines where four corners touch,
and nothing happens. A point is a period,
an intersection, spore, center of a circle,
or—"Where are my honeymoon panties?"
a woman mutters, rummaging in her purse—
the beginning of a vector in any direction.

5

The Hubble telescope spots a firefly from ten thousand
miles away. Consciousness is an infinite net

in which each hanging jewel absorbs and reflects
every other. A dog licks her fur, and a green fly

pops out; *homeless*—a teenage girl at a stoplight;
when he ignites yellow cedar in a woodstove,

the float house tilts; they aborted their twins,
and he was forced to bury them by the Mekong River.

Herringbone pattern of bricks on a bathroom floor.
Exhale: spring into sleet here now bursts—

in this world, we walk barefoot on embers, gazing
at irises; she adjusts the light and scrapes plaque

off his teeth; he sips *green snail* tea and discerns
coincident crystals: they tore off each other's clothes—

dipping apple slices into honey, they take a first bite—
inhale: here sleet into spring now bursts.

6

If you light a citronella candle, mosquitoes
can't smell you. A neighbor analyzes air
vectors to prepare a response to a dirty
bomb. Flame on a lake. Diagnosed
with Parkinson's, a man gives notice
to his wife to vacate the husk of their home.
Have I acted without body? You admire
blossoming red yarrow, but a child comes
along and uproots it. After an aneurysm,
a basket restorer leans on a cane at his ex-
wife's funeral; smoke issues from his wrists,
and he barks, "Be wind, flame." Shaggy
manes push up through grass near a sandbox.
A daughter gives her father a tin flamingo.
During the night, a raccoon lifts the lid
to a compost can, eats. Before first light
strikes the apricots on branches,
you limn human acts in the visible world.

7

Smashing a jewelry case with
    a hatchet, he grabs a necklace
        from the splintered glass and races

into oblivion. Oblivion is also
    digging up carrots in cool
        pungent air, cottonwoods branching

along the river into yellow flame;
    it's in tropical rain where four
        thousand people in an amphitheater,

swaying under umbrellas, chant
    poesía, poesía—to the far left
        and right two streams cascade the steps:

Vietnamese, English, Hindi,
    and Spanish ozone the air.
        A warm, waxy light flows across

their skin as they make the rough
    silk of love; last night
        he gazed at the curve of her eyelids

while she slept. A tiny spider
    hangs a web between a fishing
        rod and thermostat; a biologist

considers how hydra then algae
        then frogs repopulate
                a lake covered in volcanic ash;

vultures yank on a buffalo;
        somewhere a chigger acts
                as a vector of scrub typhus.

8

An architect conceived a rectangular pool
inlaid with stones, and, on three sides,
windows in the building, from ankle
to knee level, pass reflections of sky.
Looking east to the opening, you find
this slit of dreams can't be repeated.
Someone sneezes; a veterinary surgeon,
bicycling to work, is slammed by a car
into a coma. You try shifting the slant
of your pen, the strokes of your ink,
recall when you flung a tea bowl onto
the sidewalk then tried to glue the shards
together. Now hammerhead sharks
whirlpool inside you; in the volcanic
shapes of clouds, visible time; to the driver
who brakes at a red light but rear-ends
his vehicle, the driver shouts, "Horse piss!"

9

—Follow a slate path: you do not come
    to an entrance but encounter another blank wall—
I need walls to destroy walls—I ache to give
    people ~~azalea~~ persimmon emptiness,
so they can be lit from within: if I place a small

square window in the corner at floor level,
    if water spills off a cantilevered roof slab
onto a pool, and you ~~see~~ hear—wait:
    what is my grandmother, whisking tea,
saying with her hands: *this is no park*

where bones and teeth are scattered in the grass—
    I need to treat my cast-in-place concrete
like ~~sea urchin~~ a folding paper screen—a white
    gravel path leads you past another ~~concrete~~ screen—
so it's about walls, light, silencing the noise

of trucks and yells in the street—someone
    once stuck a Concealed Firearms Prohibited
sign near my recessed entrance—I detest
    bayonets—I need a keyless key—you come
to a ~~circular~~ oval lotus pond, and, in the center—

~~straw mushrooms rise into the visible world~~—
    is a stairway that descends to the entrance—
you step into an ~~alcove~~ foyer where, facing
    a blank wall, you sit, and, at sunset, *light*
sinks in and grazes your shoulders from behind—

10

The sky lightens behind the heart-shaped
leaves. While we slept, a truck filled
with plutonium lumbered down the highway.
At six a.m. the willow branches swing,
and I tilt on waves. I will tilt when I rake
gravel, uncoil a hose, loosen the spigot.
Green are the lilac and willow leaves;
now my tongue runs along your scar,
our sighs bead, and we wick into flame.
Reflected on glass, a row of track lights
is superimposed on cordate leaves
outside the window. A smallmouth bass
aligns with a cottonwood shadow
in the pond. To wait is to ache, joy,
despair, crave, fret, whirl, bloom, relax
at the unfolding center of emptiness.
I tilt on the outgoing tide of my breath.

11

"Dead? How can that BE?"
　　　a woman sobs as
　　　　　the airplane taxis to the gate;

flames on water; the whir
　　　of a hummingbird behind my eyelids;
　　　　　these are means

by which we live: joy, grief, delight—
　　　straw mushrooms
　　　　　rising into the visible world;

wisps of rabbitbrush are all
　　　that remain of generals' dreams;
　　　　　a branch of a river rejoins a river;

flip a house and it's shelter,
　　　　flip it again and cabinets
　　　　　　open, wine is poured, dogs yap,

people joke and laugh;
　　　sandhill cranes swirl
　　　　　and descend into a cornfield;

we ampere each other;
　　　a bus stops: a child gets off,
　　　　　starts walking on a red-clod road:

nothing in sight
        in all directions;
                a rose flame under our skin,

hummingbird whirring its wings;
        a rose flame,
                nothing in sight, in all directions:

Acknowledgments

Grateful acknowledgment is made to the editors of the following publications in which these poems, sometimes in earlier versions, first appeared:

Alhambra Poetry Calendar: "The Infinity Pool"

American Poet: "Comet Hyakutake"

Black Renaissance Noire: "Windows and Mirrors"

Conjunctions: "Available Light," "The Immediacy of Heat"

Connotation Press: "Windows and Mirrors"

Critical Quarterly (U.K.): "Confetti"

Denver Quarterly: "Spectral Hues"

Explosion Proof: "The Radius of Touch"

Field: "2'33"," "Midnight Loon"

The Kenyon Review: "After a New Moon," "Returning to Northern New Mexico after a Trip to Asia," "The Unfolding Center"

Malpaís Review: "Compass Rose," "The Curtain," "Orchid Hour," "Red Breath"

Mānoa: "Arctic Circle," "The Infinity Pool," "Point Blank"

Molossus: "Sarangi Music"

Narrative: "Qiviut"

The New Republic: "Fault Lines"

Orion: "Backlit"

Plume: "Glimmer Train," "Strike Slip"

Poem A Day (Academy of American Poets/Poets.org): "At the Equinox," "Comet Hyakutake," "Morning Antlers"

A Ritual to Read Together: Poems in Conversation with William Stafford, ed. Becca Lachman: "After a New Moon"

Talk Poetry: Poems and Interviews with Nine American Poets, ed. David Baker: "After a New Moon," "Returning to Northern New Mexico after a Trip to Asia"

TriQuarterly: "The Curvature of Earth," "Sarangi Music"

The Unfolding Center was published as a collaboration with Susan York by Radius Books.

"Sarangi Music" appears untitled: its thirty one lines occur in segments of one, two, three, four, five, seven, and nine lines in between other poems.

I am grateful to the Witter Bynner Foundation for Poetry for support in writing this book.

Thank you Mei mei Berssenbrugge, Jon Davis, Dana Levin, Carol Moldaw, Jim Moore, and Michael Wiegers for close readings of these poems.

Notes

P. 9

I first heard that å i åa ä e ö, in Swedish, means *island in the river* from the Dutch poet
K. Michel. The Norwegian writer Dag Straumsvåg sourced this all vowel sentence to
Swedish poet Gustaf Fröding's "Dumt Fôlk" (Stupid People). Thanks to David
Caligiuri and Connie Wanek.

P. 12

A sarangi is a short necked string instrument of India and of all the East Indian instru
ments, it is said to most resemble the sound of the human voice.

P. 34

Yerba mansa is a perennial flowering plant (*Anemopsis californica*). In New Mexico, people
boil the roots to make a medicinal tea.

P. 36

A leograph is a mythical lion figure.

P. 55

"The Unfolding Center," in collaboration with twenty two graphite drawings by Susan
York, will be exhibited at the Santa Fe Art Institute in December 2013.

P. 55

Green snail spring (*Bi Luo Chun*) is a green tea that comes from the Dong Ting mountain
region in Jiangsu, China. Picked in early spring, the leaves are rolled into a tight spiral and
resemble snail meat.

P. 67

"Flip a house and it's shelter" and the following three lines are based on an interview with
Santa Fe architect Trey Jordan.

About the Author

Arthur Sze is the author of nine books of poetry. He is also a translator and editor and has published *The Silk Dragon: Translations from the Chinese* and edited *Chinese Writers on Writing*. His poems have been translated into ten languages, including Burmese, Chinese, Dutch, Italian, and Spanish. His honors include the 2013 Jackson Poetry Prize, a Guggenheim Fellowship, and a Lannan Literary Award. A professor emeritus at the Institute of American Indian Arts, as well as a chancellor of the Academy of American Poets, Sze was the first poet laureate of Santa Fe, where he lives with his wife, Carol Moldaw, and daughter, Sarah.

Poetry is vital to language and living. Since 1972, Copper Canyon Press has published extraordinary poetry from around the world to engage the imaginations and intellects of readers, writers, booksellers, librarians, teachers, students, and donors.

WE ARE GRATEFUL FOR THE MAJOR SUPPORT PROVIDED BY:

THE PAUL G. ALLEN
FAMILY FOUNDATION

golden
lasso

Lannan

THE MAURER FAMILY
FOUNDATION

 National
Endowment
for the Arts
arts.gov
ART WORKS.

WASHINGTON STATE
ARTS COMMISSION

Anonymous

John Branch

Diana and Jay Broze

Beroz Ferrell & The Point, LLC

Janet and Les Cox

Mimi Gardner Gates

Gull Industries, Inc.
on behalf of William and Ruth True

Mark Hamilton and Suzie Rapp

Carolyn and Robert Hedin

Steven Myron Holl

Lakeside Industries, Inc.
on behalf of Jeanne Marie Lee

Maureen Lee and Mark Busto

Brice Marden

H. Stewart Parker

Penny and Jerry Peabody

John Phillips and Anne O'Donnell

Joseph C. Roberts

Cynthia Lovelace Sears and Frank Buxton

The Seattle Foundation

Dan Waggoner

Charles and Barbara Wright

The dedicated interns and faithful
volunteers of Copper Canyon Press

To learn more about underwriting Copper Canyon Press titles,
please call 360-385-4925 ext. 103

The Chinese character for poetry is made up of two parts: "word" and "temple." It also serves as press mark for Copper Canyon Press.

The text is set in Whitman, developed from Kent Lew's studies of W.A. Dwiggins's Caledonia. Book design and composition by VJB/Scribe.

CPSIA information can be obtained at www.ICGtesting.com
Printed in the USA
LVOW06s0454220814

400250LV00003B/14/P